The Waiting Room of the Imperfect Alibis

The Waiting Room of the Imperfect Alibis

Poems by

Katrin Talbot

© 2022 Katrin Talbot. All rights reserved.
This material may not be reproduced in any form, published,
reprinted, recorded, performed, broadcast,
rewritten or redistributed without
the explicit permission of Katrin Talbot.
All such actions are strictly prohibited by law.

Cover design by Shay Culligan
Cover Image by Katrin Talbot

ISBN: 978-1-63980-197-8

Kelsay Books
502 South 1040 East, A-119
American Fork, Utah 84003
Kelsaybooks.com

When you're counting alibis and not apples, one plus one equals none
—*Margaret Millar*

Lewis Carroll's Caterpillar asks Alice, "Who are *you?*"

I've asked myself that since I was little, standing in front of the mirror, momentarily *not* a twin, just a girl and her very own reflection. This collection explores the gauze between our truths and our stories and is dedicated to all who are brave enough to ask the Caterpillar's question of themselves. And especially to Nahla, my inquisitive granddaughter, who gives just the right amount of Alice answers.

Acknowledgments

Bramble: "Aging Out"

Madison Museum of Contemporary Art performance & program: "Weight Limit"

Main Street Rag: "The Barber of Cicero"

Moss Piglet: "The Countertenor and the Platypus," "A Field Guide to Western Women," "Double Take"

New Plains Review: "Homage to Floyd O. Moe"

Ode to A Bean Project chapbook and video poem for Wormfarm Institute: "A Conversation with Three Potatoes," "A Basket of Kohlrabi"

Trouvaille Review: "Swimming with Swans," "Piccolo Warming Up"

Verse-Virtual: "Lifejacket Nightlife," "The Density of Gold"

Your Daily Poem: "Lady de Crespigny's Wisdom"

Contents

The Art of Hatching

Swimming with Swans	17
Framed	18
Ambidextrous	19
Advancement	20
Lady de Crespigny's Wisdom	21
Lifejacket Nightlife	23
Huckleberries	25
Know Thyself	26
Silence According to the Crows	27
Joan's Arc	28
In Which I Again Sleep Through a Rare Celestial Event	30
A Conversation with Three Potatoes	31
Tiger's Milk	33
In Experience	34
A History of Pink	35
I've Decided to Become an Icon	36
The Art of Hatching	37
Land's End	38
A Basket of Kohlrabi	39
Piccolo Warming Up	40

Party Games

Suspect	43
The Countertenor and the Platypus	44
Aging Out	46
Case of the Missing	47
After Yeats	49
Party Games	50
A Field Guide to Western Women	51
The Transitive Property of Tennis Balls	52

Tinkerbell Gives Girl Lessons	53
The Conjugation of Truth	54
For Instance	56
Most Eligible	57
The Waiting Room of the Imperfect Alibis	58
Pot de Crème and Its Morality	59
The Dream Janitor	60
Double Take	61

Exit Wounds

Chase	65
The Barber of Cicero	66
The Other Cello	67
Exit Wounds	68
Lucky's Standard Dilutions	69
Museum Mama, Mother's Day	70
The Swooper	72
Warning	73
Arrow	74
Weight Limit	75
Instructions for Delving	77
You as a Teacup	79
Etiquette	80
Steps in a Direction	81
The Density of Gold	82

The Art of Hatching

Swimming with Swans

Not always a
question of grace,
endurance

More often, a
song of float
and preen

And you, become
a creature of
palmate,
pass by
as a piece of
lake,

shimmering

Framed

In front of a wall of
black and white
geraniums in the
kangaroo land of
no winter,
I hold the ground
with my bare feet,
dimpled ankles,
captured in my
early wide-stance
upright moments

A chubby Brunhilde
before the ring of fire,
in my collared blouse,
enormous jumper sewn
by mummy,
my hair already assuming
an unruly outlook,
my gaze just far enough
off-camera
to begin the story

Ambidextrous

She was gentle enough—
could have rapped my knuckles—
just moved my sturdy pencil
again and again to the correct hand

I learned to ignore the call of the other
to hold a pencil

Nobody, though,
could convince my left hand
to pass the scissors
to the right, but that
was more acceptable, and
she gave up quickly

In the Old West,
I might have shot brilliantly
with both hands,
preventing my own death by
gunfire, but in my days,
just a grade school
kickball champ,
and a careful cutter of
silk

Advancement

I.

Become the path,
the mossy steps
the trim of fern

Hold dances for
the gravel

Let the deer
double cross you,
the coyote trot
upon you

Be content with
Beneath

II.

Be the hands of the clock,
your brief affair with
the pinions

III.

Be the burr no one sees,
passive, aggressive,
joined by your stemmates,
carried towards your
final act of
disperse

Lady de Crespigny's Wisdom

I was six when,
in dance class,
I learned the
basic positions
of life, dance, and
decorum

She taught us the story
of Haydn's surprise
symphony, the needling
of the dozing royalty,
the priming of the
subsequent
aural jitters

But the most valuable
lesson: three steps
forward
one step
back

And the ease
with which we mastered it,
preparing us for
love, loss, and
all the
in-betweens

On days with too much stitching,
seams, unseaming,
I find myself
looking up at the clouds,
wanting to trim them with
pinking shears,
wanting them to
stay raveled,
not un-
not fringy
nor disperse—
just for an hour,
feel a certainty while
I sip something
of comfort
and breathe,
seamlessly

Lifejacket Nightlife

In the dim lighting,
they rest on
their sizing poles,
poolside

They dream of
ancestors, cork,
heritage of save,
the big float

At sunrise, they are ready
in their rows of empty,
waiting for the next
embrace, the next
almost

There's a chord we play
in a Beethoven Symphony
where the trumpets catapult
with a seventh that pulls you
back into the sling
of the shot,
all the darker apprehension
of this world,
with a syncopation to boot

Until the resolution
to a key of uneasy triumph,
and you are flung

What is *your* pull back,
your exquisite
release?
A sunrise?
A hawk drop?

Maybe just an
imperfectly-timed

exhale

Huckleberries

In that huckleberry dream,
I was back on
Sheep Mountain,
dancing with the bears,
or at least worrying about them
as we backpacked into
the wilderness—everything was
wilderness, in my memory of
my Montana—
dreadful old rhymes helped us
through the uphill trails
Left, Left,
Left my wife and forty-nine children
in starving condition
without any gingerbread
Left, Left   Right, Right,
The captain used to say,
Now you take it, and now you have it,
and don't you give it away

Huckleberry feasts are slow and
full of repetitive fanfare,
and in the dreaming,
I had forever buckets,
a purple tongue,
and too many
dance cards
to fill

Know Thyself

Attributed to
at least a dozen
Greek sages,
it seems to hover
nicely over
Thales of Miletus

Philosopher,
mathematician,
astronomer,
engineer with eyes of
stone as far as
I can tell from all
representations

And the anecdote
proving his true self—
astronomer falling down
the well, eyes on
his beloved sky

Selves in wells—
which are you?
Astronomer or
physicist,
falling or
floating?

Silence According to the Crows

It's speckled
    like a Pollock

It's a horserace
    without the thundering

Not too much a listening
    more of a diligence,
    small talk in the elevator

And the joy of
    breaking it

Declarations of
    hawk and roadkill

Then back to the process
    of marking time,
    a rest for
    the retching

Joan's Arc

The ways she sits between
my other names,
a backwards bridge to identity

First, womb baby, then,
a few months later, twin,
always suspended, wrapped in
my twin's limbs and my
great great great grandfather's name,
and once out and swaddled,
Joan settled between sur and first,
holding together my early moments
and the past

Because I'm a martyr, I'd
joke, when people asked,
though then I knew nothing
more than her pyred image tied to
the stake

But *my* Joan holds my truths,
my secrets, quietly,
cowardly, perhaps,
compared to Joan's voices,
her strength, her destiny

My Joan smolders with
a mother's sacrifice of self,
with passionate secrets,
secret passions,
her arc between who I am and
who I was,

before I grew into the inscrutable
enchantment
of name

In Which I Again Sleep Through a Rare Celestial Event

The night before,
all the experts
shaking their heads

Clouds and more clouds
Out of luck
unless you have a private airplane
to rise above the blanket

A super blue blood moon,
not seen since 1866, and not seen
this morning by me in my pajamas

Besides, blue blood stuff
is for my kids, with
their diluted genes from
William the Conqueror,
their nasty and powerful ancestor

But back to the bloody moon
which I still can't see as I sip
my super coffee and
watch the sparrows sit
on their orbit of a birdfeeder
and play moon

A Conversation with Three Potatoes

I am wondering about
the dark, the business
of under

My dark is so full of
wonder, torment,
critical plays

Can you believe in
the sun? With all
your hearts?

The sun is my fallacy—
lights the way,
blinds me

Tell me about your music—
earthworm rumbas, the rain's
thematic developments

How much thunder is
too much thunder
in your famous eyes?

And can we talk chromosomes?
You have forty-eight,
I forty-six

Hand one over and we'll be oddly even

But back to you and your philosophies,
the potato dialectics, the stunning
arguments, your metaphysical growth

I prefer aesthetics, but be well,
thank you for your answers and get back to
the swelling and bulking

I will stand at easy attention
above your canopy
every third Tuesday

and witness

Tiger's Milk

> *Christobel Mattingley wrote her best-selling children's book* Tiger's Milk *decades ago and dedicated it to her best friend, my mother: "To Margot, who gave me the recipe."*

There were no tigers
in the outback,
but we grew up and up
on their milk,
mum's recipe,
with brewer's yeast
and molasses in
cow's milk

The stream of
blackstrap
would swirl
like a circus ride,
the clumpy yeast
breaking up
with the stir,
dissolving into a
beach at sunset

And we'd sip our
destinies,
smacking our lips,
and due to genes
and tigers,
we grew up to be
as tall as this
poem

In Experience

As far as
fencing,
I have no equipment
no knowledge
no foil
no hammer
but I do know
how to
build fortresses
around a
broken heart
and
I do know how
to
dance

A History of Pink

Here, a complicated lace
lining the shores of
the lake I swim,
ruffles on ruffles
beneath the bluffs,
the eagles, the gallant
circle of vulture

Two billion year pink, rippled
glassy quartzite that remembers

Remembers glacial advances,
a blue tumble of ice,
the scrape of rock

And today, the sands along
the shore of an ancient red ocean
now a mile deep, a mile hard, a mile pink

Who could have predicted
the romance of iron-eating
bacteria? A waltz of sediment,
a tango of trilobite

A hard blush here, a softer one there
and for history's sake,
give it a
kiss

I've Decided to Become an Icon

It's not just that I
could be wrapped in silk,
boxed, mailed,
lying in a state of
glided silence deep in
the hold of the
great ship crossing a
greater or lesser ocean
as I await my placement
in the rich darkness,
the echo's center,
above the deep solemnity
of scarved worship

It's also that as an icon,
I might harness the power of
reverence to seek a little
vengeance, as unholy as may seem
from the outside, against a high
school curriculum which
chained me to a gum-laden
desk for hours at a time while
the wrestling coach showered
us with his wisdom, his stats,
his stunning options in the realm
of Career Ed

The Art of Hatching

You don't have to be a
three thousand-year-old
Egyptian, with your mud
house ovens to know
that eggs need consistent
heat to hatch
cue mother hen, brooding

Just be me, enjoying my curl
my pipping muscle swelling
as I pierce my inner membrane
and begin the breaking out

With my snare drum taps
against taut,
pipping with my piercing,
egg-tooth sawing,
the resting, then
the push with my
stretching legs

But don't check in on
me until my down dries,
until I am fluff,
active, peeping out
my first victory,
seeking a
mother

Land's End

Water's edge
land's edge
water's end,
where I go to
take myself apart,
one ripple, one stroke
at a time, bumped by weeds,
the procreation of
my humble reflection

The pulling apart
then fusion of
all that is me, all that is
left of me for this moment

And fresh from wave surgery,
I can go home
and fly

A Basket of Kohlrabi

Arms still reaching and playing,
like a gathering, a lineup after
kindergarten recess

A little artist of a plant,
sitting above,
suggesting below,
implied states

And here, a
basket of them,
singing

Piccolo Warming Up

for Linda Pereksta

Like a seam
        ripping
Like a needle
        the pierce,
        the mend

I hear her a floor below
through the hall's intercom
as I sip coffee,
check my fastenings,
scan for
unravelings

She could be
the first part of
a sunrise,
the interruption of
night by
day,
their quiet arguments,
their kiss goodnight

Party Games

Suspect

Against the bass line of
white pine,
the maple exotique begins
her rose-peach testimony

Now blushing,
falling apart on
the stand
and you wonder if
she's been lying all through
the green seasons about
what she's done with
the missing squirrels,
about the tree she
really is in
these shorter days,
these longer nights

The Countertenor and the Platypus

Admit it . . .
you instantly saw the
connection

the unexpected combination
the awe of the
whole

as he sings the *Agnus Dei*
right through your heart

as she roughs up the
basic rules of zoology

he, with the purity of
a heaven in his chaste
voice of anomaly

she, with her unquestionable
furry unity
of bill, tail, egg

the way it
suddenly seems
it ought to
be

For years, I was the A string on
Picasso's guitar,
strummed for decades by
the old guitarist

It was a good gig—
forty hours a week with
benefits and holiday

I wearied, though,
of the questions of
his blindness
of the gazes of
exhilarated sadness

So when an opening arose
as the wolf in The Peaceable Kingdom,
I gathered my references and
got the job

So nowadays,
I lie with the lambs,
never and always
worried

Aging Out

Now that we've moved past—*maid,*
we like to call ourselves
merhags—cackling in
our water-in-motion classes
but really, we are so
relieved to stop the luring,
throw away the damn seashell bras,
sport a crisp haircut

We've moved into our
manatee stage and
we're fine with that

Some of us have started
rock bands back at the grotto,
some teach sea glass mosaics,
but these days,
most of us
just mer

Case of the Missing

The sky was
pocked by
a dative hawk
and an accusative
murder of crow

Case of
who saw what
when and
then,
where

In these cases,
though,
hawks always
have alibis as
big as a
sky,
cloudy

Today, I wrote
thirteen letters to
myself—
five love letters,
three letters of outrage,
an letter of intent,
two threats of cutout letters
and two hypothetical resignations

All in all,
a busy,
penciled
day

After Yeats

I had stumbled
over his unlabeled dreams,
my gaze up on
the wild swans,
the tolling of their flight

And now we stood in
line at the butcher's in
Howth, as he watched
the folding of the butcher paper
around his selection
as if it were
an unstructured sonnet
and off he went,
parcel under his arm

I was next and
decided on chops,
after Yeats

Party Games

We've pinned the tail
on the donkey,
maybe peeking, maybe not,
ripped open presents,
gilded paper hiding truths,
eaten too much cake,
cried at popped balloons,
and now it's naptime,
the place now where
donkeys hound us,
cakes explode and
we tiptoe across floors
covered with presents
tied in impossible knots

We wake,
remember rings around
rosies, monkeys chasing
weasels, and that,
waiting for us,
there's still cake for
dessert and
the delightful possibility
of icing lipstick

A Field Guide to Western Women

The table of contents,
made of lightning-struck
bristle cone, has many
place settings

One side for wearers of chaps,
the other for lace leggings

Everyone is wearing boots

Altars to the Anasazi women
bookend the candlelit room
and the swinging saloon doors
guarantee an easy exit,
no push or pull inquiries

A moment of silence for
the silenced

And then the dig-in—
grainy dishes of landownership,
savory liberal divorce laws,
and finally, the crème de la crème,
served on a bed of
fresh juniper berries,
the right to
vote

The Transitive Property of Tennis Balls

In the dryer
three tennis balls in
tied socks are
playing a game with
the down comforter,
drumming in two four
with a pickup note

Because tennis balls are constant
and there are two sides to
an equation,
tennis balls are percussion—
at least this morning—
percussion is essential in
Beethoven's Ninth,
therefore,

Tinkerbell Gives Girl Lessons

I never got them
so this morning as I faced face
in the looking glass,
finding myself, as always, in an
empty hall staring at an
upside-down room number,
I summoned from memory Tinkerbell's techniques—
the way her lashes to fly up
like bats outtah hell,
and how a shrug and a clap could get her
whatever she wanted. And after the little
vixen herself showed up when I unconsciously
shrugged, I wondered how,
with all the sulking,
she could avoid those dastardly frown lines.
She confessed that a Disney diet takes care of any wrinkle depth.
She left before telling me
her lipstick colour code, and whether
lip liners were necessary in the best definition
of a pout, so be prepared the next time you think
you might have a possible fleeting encounter
with me and my pout,
for I might present, in my visage,
an uncoded visual rage aria
to the unprotected eye

The Conjugation of Truth

You might say truth
is not a verb,
not inflectable
but these days,
truth is
tractable, pliable,
derived, at best

I could conjugate
truthing in Basque,
with its hundreds of
possibilities for
each verb

But honestly,
I'd rather we just
go for a meander
in the falling October forest
and talk about
the trendiest flavors
of hyperbole
while we leap over
blazing puddles,
laughing

Today,
the crows had a different message

In Latin caw all morning,
relentless chanting

How that came to be
I can only guess,
guess with the faint memory of
a pile of old medical textbooks
perched on an upside down couch
up the block

Last week it was
a Stravinsky score they were
wrestling with
up in the grove of oak

The week before,
revisiting the arguments of
the devil and Daniel Webster,
when the little free library's door was
left open

But Latin seemed more suited
to their profession of
anatomical analysis,
so I enjoyed their lectures
as I raked leaves in 5/4

For Instance

Such a lovely word that
so often must,
bumping along behind
her at an alarming volume,
drag gossip and judgments,
a tinker of suggestions,
of lists,
of veritable faults uncorrected
and invisible,
thank god,
to most

Most Eligible

I saw them on the cover
of the city's glossy own,
a row of peacocks and tigers,
and wondered about
the Fortress of Eligible,
with its double moats
and dragons

Qualified to be chosen,
with megaphone and over-perfect lighting,
yet still non-partnered,
even with all those titles

Is it mother issues,
over-developed hunting instincts,
or the party boy path of
least resistance?

Of course they look delicious,
lit with that entitlement,
but I imagine they all,
deep down, just taste like
chicken

The Waiting Room of the Imperfect Alibis

They have had their day in court,
avoiding the fessing,
transforming the facts,
and now they sit,
waiting to be called for their
morality root canals,
dissections of their Elsewhere glands
and vaccinations of truth serum
as they aimlessly flip through the glossies,
redesigning their imaginary whereabouts,
their imaginary lives, all nine of them,
as they wait for their name to be called,
the corrosion in their brass tacks
revealed

Pot de Crème and Its Morality

With an exposed description
as a "loose French
dessert custard"
dating from the 1600s,
how is one supposed to
feel about dipping into
the tiny pot,
savouring spoonful by
naughty spoonful?

And then, one, as a household
cook, must consider family
values when planning menus—
a loose French dessert
has no place
in a child's world, so go ahead and
make the Serves Four

The top shelf of the fridge is
an excellent hiding place behind the
bottles of probiotics and spicy mustards

You are protecting your children's
emotional development—
schedule consumption
after their bedtime

The Dream Janitor

He had no idea, apparently
about the burden ahead
when I hired him
but what did he expect?
He must have known about
my messy messy days,
the tiger training sessions,
bear wrestling,
the charming of the snakes
—I had a reputation, after all,
and the sparkly spandex uniforms
all over the house,
the sequins stuck in the rug,
should have been a dead
give-away
What does he have to
complain about?
I pay him well,
on the condition that he
supply his own old-world broomsticks
and Medusa mops
It's a job, for godssakes,
with benefits, and though I'm a
challenging employer,
my heart is big,
my respect for hard work deep,
and, despite my wild life,
I'm rooted in clean dirt,
and don't ever spill my milk,
even while riding a
pizza at 72 mph

Double Take

I'll be your anything

Anything for you—
the burning building, car-leaping
horse-bucking, balcony-falling

Wrap all your harnesses and
wires around me
I know how it feels to be
edited

Call me your stunt double,
dance double, trouble double

But remember,
I have more freckles,
better legs,
and a paycheck
to die for

Exit Wounds

Chase

What if I chased your
car like a dog—
ears back, flat out run,
barking in 7/4?

You'd turn on your matchbox siren,
your blue and red stage lights,
floor it, peel away from
the mutt I have become

I'd laugh and cry
and realize you've become
your own kind of dogged,
your own kind of
howl

The Barber of Cicero

It was hair-raising tale
she told me in the Y locker room
Aldo, her sister's father-in-law,
a barber until his 90s,

when he retired the scissors,
his eyes tired of managing
the necessary symmetry
of that expected in a haircut

Back in the motherland,
he had been a child prodigy—
Age eleven, the Italian boy was
sent to cut the hair of nuns,
snipping away the sensuous curls,
the light and saintly split ends

A ship brought him across the ocean
to Cicero, America
where he eventually set up shop

And had Mr. Al Capone at
his mercy on a regular basis,
scissors, razors near his throat,
trimming away at the power

Remembering, sometimes,
the almighty silence of
his earliest sculptures,
the benevolence of his beloved nuns

The Other Cello

We're used to it,
our foggy role as the little sister
to everybody's favorite,
or as the big awkward sister to
the bombshell,
the butt of jokes so true they tickle,
the simpleton implications
woven into our parts beleaguered
with penciled fingerings,
desperate accidentals
as we face the Alto clef challenge in the
World of Treble-Bass

But look carefully, will you,
the next time you attend
a symphony concert . . .
As we warm up, who is the
happiest? We the violists let our egos
float downstream years ago,
so we're not, in general, desperate to
drown out our stand partner
with flashy passage-work, nor,
with furrowed brow, are
we inclined to consult fingerboard
roadmaps with another cellist.
We're content to settle in,
after hearing the latest
toddler or puppy report,
to become an inner voice as the
most delicious mustard
you've ever slathered on a
a sandwich of tonality

Exit Wounds

The parting shot
could have been classier,
a bullet point of wisdom,
compassion,
but I understand—
you have your own
time signature
and we're all going
through key changes,
minor and major,
some of us still
humming

Lucky's Standard Dilutions

Hot coffee
Sunshine
Heart that shatters and mends
Paychecks
Just enough chickens in my backyard
Sunshine
Heart that mends and shatters
No broken bones
Hot coffee
Heart that mends and mends
Lap of cat
Sunshine
Heart that shatters and
shatters

Museum Mama, Mother's Day

Andrea Vanni, 1375
the Mourning Madonna

I'm not talking about
the shhhhh species,
the ones who try to keep the spirit cultured
while the sweet conversant baby
in the backpack
drools away awe,
dismisses landscapes with loud jabber,
drops pacifiers instead of names
in the somber galleries

It's the mother hidden
in a corner,
her haunting gray green pallor
the color of grief,
the listless beauty of
her empty hands,
the unfathomable rich sadness
garnered in her eyes,
as if just last month
she had lost a son

I wanted to brush her fingers,
touch her cheek,
but the guards would have
come running,
so I left her alone
in her sad gilded world,
ornately framed by the age-old story,
her only comfort 600 years ago,

the brush of the artist,
who named her
the Mourning Madonna

The Swooper

Daughter,
stuck, captive,
all those chains
All I needed was a car
and my t-shirt with
William Morris's
words

Love is All

I drove up, walked in
in the dark,
backed up by
the idling power company guys,
my basso continuo safety net
standing by,
and I
swooped

Warning

> *the one no one dares win*
> —Richard Hugo

The wall that always stands
between concept and memory

Never a gauzy view
of the other

Stone, usually, laid and built by
the blind, brilliantly, slowly by touch

Each edge of misconception
fitted into the next

Until enough is enough,
high enough, wide enough

The inlaid barbs shining in
hatred's piercing gaze,

Ready for the battle,
the one no one dares win

Arrow

His middle name,
waif of a boy
lived down the road
through the ponderosas
edge of the range
our next door neighbors
a mile's third away
His eyes, wide wide,
gathering each fine miracle,
The first snow,
the glacier lily's stunning fanfare
this summer's dusty piney day
We knew his trajectory,
short, sweet
as the disease gathered
his breath slowly, the crack of his cough
always a bitter comma in the moments
of childhood—a tight reminder of
a life's pacing off
We moved away,
he didn't grow in our memory
but his country boy sweetness
swelled in recollection
A few years later we heard
by mail of his final ellipsis,
a few sad sentences
lined with the relief
of loving

Weight Limit

A response to a Do Ho Suh exhibit at the Madison Museum of Contemporary Art

The houses I carry
in my head—
without foundation,
without shingles

Spinning slowly on this
massive ephemeral turntable,
singing the canticles of
settled, of
Inside

It's the light in each room I
remember—how I
could breathe, embrace the
other, the outside in
some rooms, but not others—
Which rooms to walk in,
through, which to sit in,
to lie
And what happened where,
which drew a memory cage
around each room,
There, where my father fainted—
a kidney stone—hit his head on
the Canadian sink,
blood on porcelain,
Or there down under,
where I awoke, mid-air,
in my fall from the top bunk
Or the little kitchen in Bonn,

where my mother built
the gingerbread house out of
our dreams and gave it away
to charity, to some other family to
savor, demolish, digest
The ups and downs
of a home,
the sheer bones
that stay unburied when we
leave

Instructions for Delving

Forgo the forgone

Believe that parchment and promises
are iron of a kind that flakes quickly,
falls out of handles, helpless,
like a shovel blade left
in the woods

Write sonnets in the rust
about friable hearts you have known

Take up gardening
Plant only regrets
Make a point of
harvesting too early

Become conclusive
Conclude with becoming

Always need more less

It's always something to
do with bones
And this morning, on the prairie, as
I turned my back on the pile of
them, gilded with fur,
they began to realign themselves

I could hear the return
to order, a structural canon
of the spine's brackets,
the echoes of femurs
sounding a path,
the tiniest bones asserting
themselves in a
complicated plainsong

What can we say about death
that can be heard,
that sticks to our soul's
denying,
about the beauty in
a cage of bones,
the necessary *chant du cygne*
as one life parts from another?

You as a Teacup

When did you turn
to porcelain
chipped, stained,
perfect for holding what is needed
Your cracked glaze witness to
a half century of delicate duty,

a shattering,
the slow rebuilding,
articulated sorrow
sketched into your vessel on a
tea-stained canvas of brittle,
unfathomable strength

Be sure to glue the handle back
on upside down
because that is
the right way now to
find a grip

Etiquette

Howling is not lady-like,
Crawling improper,
so finish the dishes.
make the beds

and follow me, at midnight,
over the dunes where
we'll crawl in 4/4 time

We'll go down
by the tracks
and wait for
the engines to chug over
our bellows

Smile, they say.
Show your teeth

Find the roar
behind your
lipstick

Steps in a Direction

It wasn't necessarily the right
day to migrate—tornado warning—
but we went ahead anyway
with our shower caps,
picnic basket and a wheelbarrow
of locks and keys

The chickens and goats had to stay but
we left the coop open and
colouring books inside

Brought the typewriter,
cello, accordion,
left the piccolo

Put the mirrors on the curb and
packed the sparrows

We were in a hurry but
we threw away all the clocks

It was time to lose count

The Density of Gold

I had harvested a
handful of goldfinch
along yards of a path slicing
through the prairie.
No sweet feet holding the
final songs, just
feathers and

feathers.

Who knew how much gold
it took to fly?

About the Author

Australian-born Katrin Talbot's collection *The Devil Orders a Latte* is forthcoming from Fernwood Press, and she has seven chapbooks, including *Wrong Number, The Blind Lifeguard,* and *Freeze-Dried Love* from Finishing Line Press; *Attached—Poetry of Suffix, The Little Red Poem,* and *noun'd, verb* from dancing girl press; and *St. Cecilia's Daze* from Parallel Press. Her poetry has appeared in many journals, including *Main Street Rag, Trouvaille Review, Fresh Ink, Bramble,* and *Your Daily Poem* and many anthologies. She also has two Pushcart Prize nominations and quite a few chickens.

www.ingramcontent.com/pod-product-compliance
Lightning Source LLC
Chambersburg PA
CBHW030911170426
43193CB00009BA/813